D1276638

CRYPTOLOGISTS

Life Making and Breaking Codes

Aaron Rosenberg

The Rosen Publishing Group, Inc., New York

Published in 2004 by The Rosen Publishing Group, Inc.
29 East 21st Street, New York, NY 10010

Library of Congress Cataloging-in-Publication Data

Rosenberg, Aaron.
Cryptologists : life making and breaking codes / by Aaron
Rosenberg.—1st ed.
    p. cm. — (Extreme careers)
Summary: Examines the careers available in the field of
cryptology, discussing the necessary education, training, and
on-the-job duties.
Includes bibliographical references and index.
ISBN 0-8239-3965-0 (lib. bdg.)
1. Cryptography—Vocational guidance—Juvenile literature.
[1. Cryptography—Vocational guidance. 2. Vocational
guidance.] I. Title. II. Series.
Z103.3.R67 2003
652'.8'023—dc21

                                        2002153685

Manufactured in the United States of America

Contents

Introduction: Secrets and Spies

The term "cryptology" comes from the Greek word for "hidden writing." It is the science of disguised communication, the art of making and breaking codes. Cryptology has two sides: cryptography, which is the making of codes, and cryptanalysis, which is the breaking (figuring out) of codes. Cryptology requires a lot of math, but it is far more exciting than most mathematics, because the cryptologist pits his or her wits against other people. It's also an important field; cryptologists have affected the outcomes of both world wars and other conflicts as well.

Cryptology is also used by many businesses today to secure their computer systems. And we all

At the National Cryptologic Museum in Fort Meade, Maryland, a Korean War veteran examines a display explaining the United States's use of cryptanalysis during that conflict.

know how the Internet uses cryptology: Encryption is used every time you go to a "secure" site, which was built by a cryptologist.

Curious about what it takes to be a real cryptologist? Read on, and crack the code!

Codes and Ciphers

odes have been used since almost the beginning of history. Most codes have been used by the military. Julius Caesar, dictator of Rome, created his own cipher in 50 BC to be able to communicate secretly with his generals. Today, codes are used by both the military and businesses to protect information and communications.

The first thing to know about cryptology is that there are ciphers and there are codes. The two are not the same. Both hide a text's true meaning, but they work differently. Ciphers hide the meaning by replacing letters with other symbols, for instance using other letters or numbers. Codes replace whole words or phrases. You and your friends have used a cipher if you've written notes to each other that replaced each letter of the alphabet with the next letter in sequence. For example, a cipher can replace the letters for "apple" with "bqqmf." Likewise, you create a code by replacing words with phrases, numbers, or symbols, so that, for instance, "homework" becomes the number 7, and "too much" is replaced by the word "blue." When we talk about code making and code breaking, however, we mean both codes and ciphers.

Making and Reading Codes and Ciphers

Julius Caesar developed the first recorded cipher in 50 BC. Although very simple, it served as the basis of many ciphers to come.

All codes and ciphers work the same way. They always take a text and encode or encrypt it so that no

Code Talkers

Codes are similar to languages. Words, phrases, and symbols have meanings, and they can be strung together to form sentences and ideas. One of the strongest codes ever used was an actual language. During World War II, the United States Marines used "code talkers," Navajo Indians trained to transmit information using a coded version of the Navajo language. Navajo is an extremely complex language, and it is only spoken, never written. This meant that no one would have a Navajo dictionary on hand. A code talker could encode, transmit, and decode a three-line English message in twenty seconds. The same job took the best computers of the time half an hour. More than four hundred Navajo served as code talkers during the war. According to later reports from the Japanese chief of intelligence, the Japanese never managed to crack the code.

These Navajo code talkers receive and decode a message while in the field.

unwanted person can read it. The intended recipient decodes or decrypts the message. Both sides have a key, which tells them exactly how to convert the text. In a simple system, both sides use the same key—you and your friend both know that "blue 7" means "too much homework" because you know the same code. The problem with this type of simple coding is that anyone who intercepts it at either end can figure out what the text means. Let's see how.

The cipher that Julius Caesar developed is extremely simple. All he did was replace every letter with the letter three places further down in the alphabet. Thus, "a" becomes "d," and "apple" becomes "dssoh." This is the Caesar substitution cipher. It's a simple substitution because the letters always move the same way—once you realize that "d" in the encrypted text represents "a," you can move every letter forward three positions and read the message.

In the fifteenth century, an Italian named Leon Battista Alberti came up with ciphers that were more difficult by

Besides inventing the cipher disk, Alberti was also an architect, musician, philosopher, painter, and sculptor.

African American Slave Quilts

Cryptology can be used to preserve freedom by protecting identities and secrets. One of the most inspiring stories is the creation of slave quilts in the early and mid-1800s. Secret messages embedded in the quilts assisted slaves from the American South in their efforts to escape to freedom in the North. Quakers began the Underground Railroad in 1780, and by 1830, it had achieved legendary status among those who sought to escape slavery. "Conductors" helped the passengers get to border points such as Cincinnati, Ohio, and Wilmington, Delaware, or to Great Lake ports such as Detroit, Michigan, or Buffalo, New York, for quick passage to Canada. In order for the Underground Railroad to work effectively, conductors had to get messages to would-be passengers without being caught. They created a system based on designs sewn into quilts. The quilts looked normal and could be displayed openly. To those who knew, the symbols on the quilts could reveal a great deal. For example, a monkey wrench design meant it was time to gather whatever was needed for the journey, and sailboat designs meant boats were available. Quilts were also used to indicate safe houses, or hiding places along the Underground Railroad's route.

inventing the cipher disk. A cipher disk has a circle with all the letters of the alphabet on it and a second smaller circle with either letters or numbers. The two circles are fastened together through the center, so that the smaller circle can rotate freely. If you and your friend decide that "a" equals "s," you turn the smaller circle until its "s" lines up with the "a" on the larger circle. All the other letters have a match as well, and this is your code.

A simple cipher disk has the letters in order on both wheels, but they can be mixed up on the smaller wheel to make the code more secure ("g" might come after "s" on the smaller wheel, so that "a" becomes "s" but "b" becomes "g"). This is known as polyalphabetic substitution, because the substitutions are not fixed to a single set (in the Caesar method, "a" is always "d"). Most decoder rings and decoder badges found in cereal boxes are cipher disks.

In 1867, Charles Wheatstone created the cryptograph. This was an

English physicist and inventor Sir Charles Wheatstone's cryptograph was a great innovation in the field of cryptography.

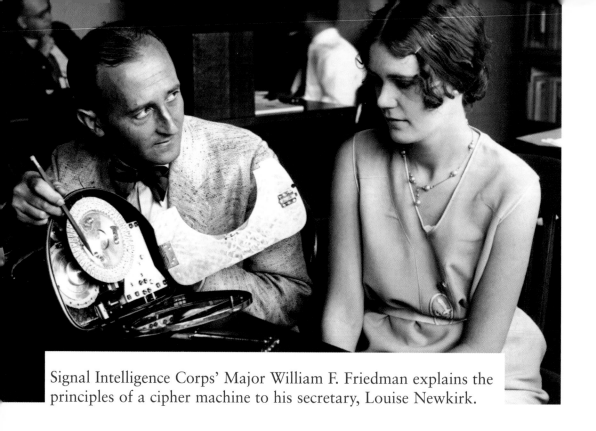

Signal Intelligence Corps' Major William F. Friedman explains the principles of a cipher machine to his secretary, Louise Newkirk.

automated cipher disk with two hands like a clock, one long and one short. Gears controlled the movement of the smaller hand so that the cipher kept changing regularly.

Mathematics and Codes

Stronger codes are usually built around an algorithm, or encryption key. This is a mathematical formula that determines how the letters are replaced. The algorithm for the Caesar substitution cipher is x + 3, or the letter that is three places past the original letter. The more complicated the algorithm, the harder it is for anyone else to decipher those messages.

Today, most codes use prime numbers (numbers divisible by only themselves and the number 1, like 1, 3, 7, 11, or 137). Some prime numbers have hundreds or even thousands of digits, so no one can possibly guess which prime you used in your message. The longer the prime, the safer the code. Some codes, with their really long prime number keys, would potentially take several thousand years to break!

Public-Key Encryption

The most recent type of encryption is called public-key encryption. Three Massachusetts Institute of Technology mathematicians—Ronald L. Rivest, Adi Shamir, and Leonard M. Adleman—created it in the mid-1970s. Basically, public-key encryption uses numbers and the prime numbers they can be factored into. For example, the factors of 15 are 5 and 3, where 5 x 3 = 15 and both 5 and 3 are primes.

Here's how this works. Alice and Bob want to send secret messages. Alice runs a computer program that randomly picks two prime numbers—in this case, 5 and 3. Then she multiplies them to get the total. This total (15) is Alice's public key. She can post this on her Web site, attach it to her e-mail, and tell it to everyone she knows.

Bob wants to send Alice a secret message. He takes his text and encrypts it, using Alice's public key as the key for the algorithm (so he plugs the number 15 into the algorithm). Then he sends the coded message to Alice. But here's the tricky part—the way the algorithm is set up, you must know both factors to decode the message. So it isn't enough to know that the encryption key is 15—you must also know that the decryption keys are 3 and 5. With these low numbers, that's easy; but if Alice's public key is a hundred digits long, even a supercomputer couldn't find the factors without a few years of computing time.

So, Alice is the only one who can decode Bob's message. This encryption is extremely secure because Alice isn't bothering to hide the encryption key—that's public. She just doesn't tell anyone the decryption keys, and no one can figure them out.

Using Public-Key and Private-Code Encryption

Most people don't use public-key encryption for messages. Why not? It takes too long to encode and decode. The computer must plug that public key or those factors into the algorithm. Instead, people use a hybrid system, part public key and part private code. Here's how.

Alice and Bob decide to exchange secret messages. Both of them have public keys. Alice comes up with a private code (maybe she decides to use prime numbers for the letters of the alphabet, so that "a" is 1, "b" is 2, "c" is 3, "d" is 5, "e" is 7, and so on). She sends Bob a message using his public key. Her message gives him the private code. Now she and Bob can send each other messages with that private prime-for-letters code. They used only their public keys to exchange the code without anyone intercepting it. There are so many possible codes available that, unless you have some idea what you're looking at, you'll never be able to solve them.

Code
Breaking

The point of a code is to keep something secret. That means the information must be important enough to hide. You wouldn't bother coding a message about what you're eating for dinner, but you might code a message about how much you hate lima beans if you don't want your mother to know. If the information is important, someone is going to want to know it. Which means someone will try to crack your code.

Cryptanalysis

The art of breaking codes and ciphers is called cryptanalysis. If you overhear Alice telling Bob the code key or you find Alice's cipher disk while it's still set to her current code, you haven't actually solved the code—you only found the information. This doesn't count as breaking a code. Cryptanalysis is about figuring out the code or cipher without already knowing the key or the algorithm. So how does this work?

Breaking Ciphers

Monoalphabetic substitutions are easy to solve. Take the Caesar substitution cipher, for example. If "d" means "a," then "r" must mean "o." Once you've figured out two letters, the rest fall into place. Even if we use the prime-number method from chapter 1, as soon as you discover that each letter is a prime number, and that the next letter is the next prime number, you've solved the code.

Polyalphabetic ciphers are much harder to decrypt because the letter matches change for each message. The best way to break a cipher is to look for letter patterns. Doubled letters are particularly helpful. Not many words use two of the same letter. You can also

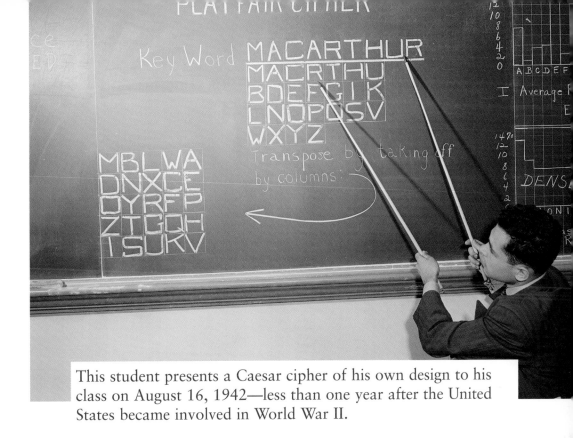

This student presents a Caesar cipher of his own design to his class on August 16, 1942—less than one year after the United States became involved in World War II.

look for more common letters. For example, vowels appear more frequently in words, especially "a," "e," and "o." The problem isn't that you cannot break a polyalphabetic cipher. It's the fact that your key might be useless next time around, because letter combinations will have been switched.

One way to beat polyalphabetic ciphers is to create a cipher disk that matches the originals. If "a" equals "d" and "o" equals "e," the cipher disk's smaller wheel probably has "a" and "o" next to each other. The larger wheel has the letters in alphabetic order. So on the next message, once you've figured out that "a" is now "r," see if "o" becomes "s." Once you know what order the letters are in, you have a complete cipher disk. Then it's just a matter of finding the right key each time. That's easy, because you have only twenty-six choices.

Breaking Codes

Codes are usually harder to break than ciphers. The words or symbols might not have anything to do with the original word. Also, there might not be a clear pattern: Why is homework translated as "7" but "too much" becomes "blue"? A good code probably doesn't have a clear pattern; the words and symbols are as random as possible. The more random they are, the harder it is for anyone else to crack the code.

The only way to beat a code is to build your own codebook. Your codebook is a dictionary, with regular words on one side and their codes on the other. Get as many messages in the code as you can find. Then look them over. Watch for words that reappear often.

The First Cryptomachine

One of the features that separates people from animals is the invention of tools. People invent devices to help them do things more easily and more quickly. Cryptology is no exception. Fredrik Gripenstierna of Sweden invented the Chiffre-Machinen and presented it to King Gustaf III in 1786. It had fifty-seven wheels, all mounted on a single shaft and housed within a cylinder. Each wheel had the alphabet engraved on one half and the numbers 0 to 99 engraved on the other. The numbers were mixed up in a different order on each wheel. Each letter of a message (which could be up to fifty-seven letters long) came from a separate wheel. The wheels were moved to show the plaintext on one side while on the opposite side of the cylinder appeared the ciphertext. The first ten wheels also had code numbers, so a message could be started at the second wheel or the fourth wheel instead of the first, for added security.

If the messages are written in normal English, the most common words will be "a," "an," and "the." If they're written like a telegraph, the most common word will be "Stop," and it'll be at the end of every sentence. If you know what a message is about, that helps. For example,

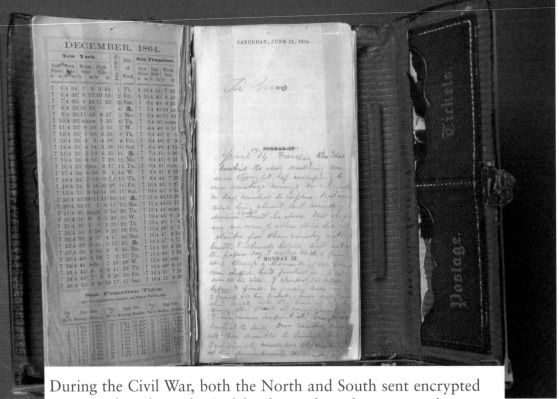

During the Civil War, both the North and South sent encrypted messages by telegraph. Codebooks, such as the one seen here, were needed to decipher the transmissions.

you know Alice and Bob were talking about homework, and you see "7" appear several times. It's a good bet that "7" refers to homework. On the other hand, if they were talking about driving around and you see "poodle" many times, it might be their code word for "car." Every time you learn what a code word means, write it into the codebook. Writing codebooks is how linguists translate ancient languages—one word at a time.

Eventually you'll find a pattern in the code. Perhaps Alice and Bob were careless and used numbers for every noun and colors for every quantifier (number). If you can find the pattern, solving the code becomes easier. You can start guessing at words. Eventually you'll be able to make sense of their messages, and that means you've broken their code.

Testing a Solved Code

A good way to test a newly solved code is to plant information. You mention to Alice that you know a used car she could buy. You're certain that she'll tell Bob, and sure enough, she sends him a coded message. The word "poodle" appears several times. That must mean "car," because you know that's what she's telling him about. What's more, the message says, "snow poodle" several times. If she's talking about the used car, and "poodle" means "car," "snow" must mean "used." So perhaps Alice and Bob use weather for adjectives. You can watch for that in later messages and see if the theory fits.

Enigma

In 1919, a Dutch man named Hugo Koch created an encryption device. This device used a normal typewriter keyboard, but the letters typed were not the letters that printed on the page. This would not have been very impressive, except that the letters changed every time they were typed. For example, if you typed "aaa" into the machine, you might get "gqr" printed on the page. This new encryption method made normal cryptanalysis useless. Anyone trying to decode the message might figure that "a" was "g," and never realize that "a" changed to

This four-rotor Enigma machine *(right)* was removed from a World War II German U-boat. Although the Germans believed the code to be unbreakable, it was cracked by British and Polish cryptographers in the early 1930s.

"q" the second time, "r" the third time, and some new letter every time after that.

Koch couldn't find any real use for his device, so he sold it to a German engineer, Dr. Arthur Scherbius. Scherbius made some improvements, named the machine Enigma, and eventually sold it to the German military. They claimed that it would take a full team several billion years to crack Enigma's code. Alan Turing of Britain and Marian Rejewiski of Poland broke the code in the early 1930s. In February 1940, the British captured a U-boat with an Enigma machine and its code-typing wheels (rotors).

Computers and Code Breaking

Computers are extremely useful for code breaking. It takes the human mind several minutes to run through all the letter combinations, but a computer can find them in seconds. Computers can also be programmed to watch for certain things, for instance doubled letters. And on a computer, several pages or messages can be put up at once, and sections can be copied back and forth.

What computers cannot do is guess. The computer doesn't know Alice and Bob, and it cannot

25

guess what they're likely to talk about on any given day. Cryptologists must supply intuition and plug in theories and systems for the computer to use. Even when dealing with algorithms, the computer can't do it alone. It can compute numbers more easily (though only smaller ones are possible, even for larger computers), but cryptologists must program it to watch for the numbers first, and to decode them in a certain way.

The computer is simply a tool, just like the cipher disk; it makes things quicker and easier for the cryptologist. Nothing can replace the personal approach. People always devise codes, even if all they do is program the computer to spit out random numbers for words. People will always be needed for decoding as well.

Learning Cryptology

Becoming a cryptologist is a challenge that most people in the field have found to be worth the effort. A cryptologist needs good math skills. Even if you're working with codes instead of ciphers, you must be good at math. Cryptology is about logic, patterns, and systems. Math is about finding solutions to problems by using logic, patterns, and systems. The connection is clear.

Cryptologists also need persistence. Most codes cannot be cracked quickly. Likewise, any code that's created in a few minutes can probably be beaten in only a few more. Creating difficult codes often takes months or years. But a good cryptologist never quits. The answer is always there; it just takes time to reach it.

The Crypto Wars

During the 1990s, the U.S. government fought its own citizens over what was known as strong crypto. This was a particular type of cipher so strong it could not be broken, even by government agencies. The legal battles became known as the Crypto Wars. People, particularly cryptologists, wanted strong crypto to ensure privacy. The government, however, worried that criminals would use the strong crypto to conceal evidence of their activities. In 1999, the people finally won the Crypto

More than 150 leaders in academia, technology, and government assembled at the SafeNet2000 Summit to discuss issues of Internet privacy. Here, Bill Gates, chairman of Microsoft, gives a keynote speech calling for greater Internet security.

Wars. The courts declared that strong crypto was a form of speech and therefore protected by the First Amendment. Oddly enough, not many people have used strong crypto since. Several cases proved that the government's fears were unnecessary—even when a criminal was smart enough to use strong crypto, he or she often forgot to protect the system properly, and the authorities were still able to access those files. Cryptologists realized the same thing themselves—no matter how strong your ciphers, if someone can gain your keys (usually on your computer), he or she can read all your files with ease.

Cryptologists must also be highly organized. They might use their instincts to help solve puzzles, but that's only to get them started in a direction. Once an idea forms, the cryptologist has to be methodical and cover every possible avenue. Otherwise, he or she might skip past the solution without even noticing. Cryptology is a science, and that means it's detail-oriented. Every combination must be tried, in a set order, and the results carefully noted. Sometimes failures can reveal as much as successes. Sometimes, a code can be broken by seeing what it doesn't do.

Cryptographic Training

For a long time, there was no formal training in cryptology. People who loved math and puzzles studied codes and ciphers on their own time. They learned how to build and break them. These people sometimes found jobs in cryptology, but for some it was only a hobby.

In the late 1920s, Poland's cipher bureau was trying to crack a new German cipher. It was not having any luck. Then it realized that mathematicians might be able to help. In 1929, the dean of mathematics at the University of Poznan provided the army with a list of his best graduating students. These students received additional training from the cipher office. This may have been the first actual class in cryptology. (The three best students in the class—Marian Rejewski, Henryk Zygalski, and Jerzy Róycki—were later important figures in cracking the Enigma code.)

Today, other schools offer programs in cryptology or related fields. The University of London's Royal Holloway College offers a master's degree in information security. The University of Leuven (in Belgium) and Waterloo University (in Canada) are both known for their cryptology courses.

Does that mean you need a degree in cryptology itself? Not really. But most cryptologists have a degree in math, and generally a focus on probability, statistics, simulations, or differential equations. Computer programming is also important so that you can set computers to run encryption and decryption programs. Engineering skills are useful,

A student at the University of Southwestern Louisiana gets a hands-on computer science lesson from an instructor. Good computer skills are essential to an aspiring cryptologist.

since cryptographic devices can be mechanical instead of computerized (or a combination of both).

Language training is also useful. As mentioned in chapter 2, breaking a code requires the same techniques as deciphering an ancient language. Likewise, understanding the way languages are built can help a person to figure out the patterns behind a current code.

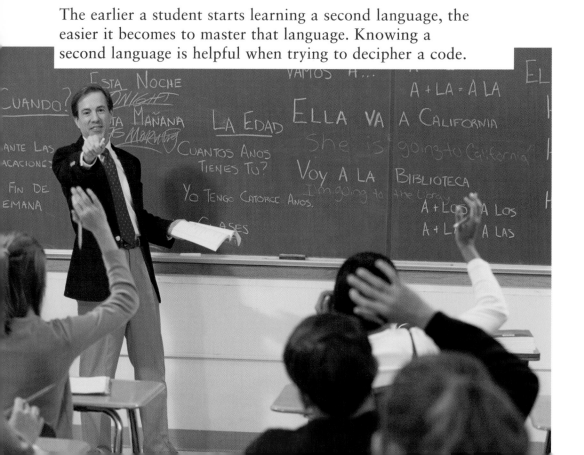

The earlier a student starts learning a second language, the easier it becomes to master that language. Knowing a second language is helpful when trying to decipher a code.

Cryptologists should also have good communication skills, both oral and written. That's because most cryptologists work in teams, and it's important to share information. If you can explain yourself clearly and quickly, others can see what you're doing and offer advice and help more easily.

U.S. Government Training Programs

Some government programs offer their own courses to new recruits. The National Security Agency (NSA) has run the Junior Officer Cryptologic Career Program (JOCCP) since 1974. This program is for junior military officers with backgrounds in cryptology. JOCCP participants take classes at the National Cryptologic School and are assigned tasks at various centers within the NSA. This gives the officers advanced knowledge and on-the-job training.

The Naval Postgraduate School (NPS) also offers training in cryptology, though only for naval officers. Officers at NPS learn electronic engineering, computer science and systems, communications, information warfare, space operations, and financial management. Mastering these skills makes the officer eligible for a variety of jobs, mainly technical and most based in Washington, D.C.

In the same way, applicants to the NSA join the Cryptanalysis Intern Program (CAIP). They attend formal classes, receive technical training from experienced cryptanalysts, and rotate to various jobs throughout the NSA. Participants can also take classes at local universities, and the NSA often finances this education.

Today, most cryptology jobs require that applicants have at least a college degree, and many insist on a graduate degree. The most common degrees for applicants are in the fields of mathematics, computer science, engineering, and linguistics. Applicants with other degrees who demonstrate strong mathematical and analytical skills are also considered. Acceptance is usually less about what

Cryptanalysis often involves the use of advanced mathematics.

your diploma says than about what you learn and how you use it.

Cryptologists see patterns and structures in everything, and they live to uncover secrets (and to cover them up again). Even a liberal arts or fine arts education can be useful in that process because it can teach the individual how to see things from a different perspective and how to analyze structures consistently.

Careers in Cryptology

So, what can you do with cryptology? It's fun, interesting, and challenging, but how does it pay the bills? Who's going to hire a cryptologist? You might be surprised at the need for cryptologists in this high-tech world in which we live.

Thirty years ago, the only place you could get a cryptology job was with the U.S. government, and particularly the NSA. Today that's all changed. Cryptology is a billion-dollar-a-year field, and it appears in every aspect of daily life. Large companies often hire cryptologists for their in-house security teams. Also, the Internet is built upon the notions of security, privacy, and access. And of course, the U.S. government is still a major employer as well.

Government

The government is supposed to protect its citizens from all threats, foreign and domestic. In order to do that, it needs information about those threats. The more information the government has, the better job it can do of protecting its citizens. Intelligence is a major portion of every government branch, from the military to the legislature to the courts.

A U.S. Navy cryptologic technician prepares leaflets to be dropped over Iraq in December 2002. The leaflets list radio frequencies at which Iraqis can hear information about the presence of the United Nations in their country.

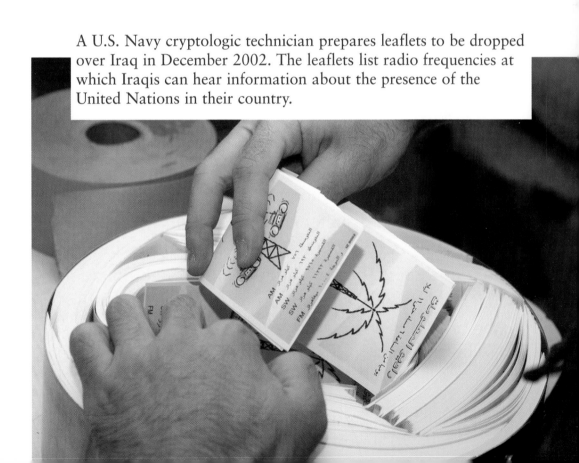

Not everyone wants their information to be read, or even found, particularly if someone can use it against them. Why tell people your weaknesses or broadcast your failures? So, people often hide the details. Or, if they're talking to others about it, they encode the information. And this is where cryptologists come in.

Of course, the U.S. government doesn't want all its secrets to come out either, especially to foreign powers. So, government information must be protected. Important communications are encoded to prevent foreign interception. And that requires a cryptologist as well.

Each branch of the military has its own intelligence division. If possible, coded transmissions from enemies (and sometimes allies) are intercepted and decoded. Officers trained for these jobs know general intelligence, cryptology, or both. Intelligence officers can be dispatched to a location within the United States or in a foreign land to acquire information firsthand. They might also sift through materials back at headquarters. Important information within the branch is encoded by the intelligence division and made as secure as possible.

NSA

The single largest employer of cryptologists is the National Security Agency (NSA). This intelligence agency is responsible for all governmental communications in the United States and for monitoring the communications of foreign powers. Cryptanalysis is a core discipline, and the NSA is always looking for talented cryptologists to join its team. The NSA provides

The NSA's Web page, located at http://www.nsa.gov, provides a link where you can download a free version of the Linux operating system with security enhancements.

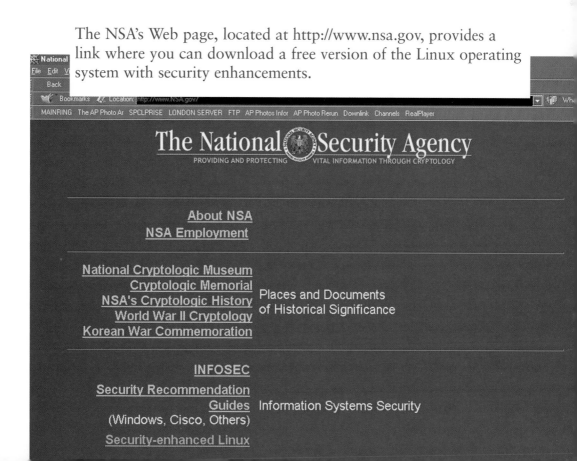

The National Security Agency

PROVIDING AND PROTECTING VITAL INFORMATION THROUGH CRYPTOLOGY

About NSA
NSA Employment

National Cryptologic Museum
Cryptologic Memorial
NSA's Cryptologic History   Places and Documents
World War II Cryptology   of Historical Significance
Korean War Commemoration

INFOSEC
Security Recommendation
Guides   Information Systems Security
(Windows, Cisco, Others)
Security-enhanced Linux

intelligence reports to the nation's leaders and is constantly examining information for anything that might be important or become important.

The NSA's headquarters are located in Maryland at Fort George G. Meade, about thirty miles northeast of the Central Intelligence Agency's (CIA) headquarters. This is the command center for the largest and most sensitive intelligence-gathering apparatus in the world. More than fifteen thousand employees work here.

The NSA was founded in 1972, although it grew out of two earlier organizations: Military Intelligence Section 8 (or MI-8) from World War I and the American Black Chamber (also known as the Code Compilation Company), which operated from 1919 to 1929. The NSA is responsible for the security of U.S. government communications, called COMSEC, or communications security. It also breaks foreign codes and monitors any and all communications around the world. This is called SIGNIT, or signals intelligence. All information is passed along to other intelligence agencies and to the White House. The three major offices of the NSA are the Office of Signal Intelligence (which studies the actual signals sent, in terms of location and type), the Office of Communication Security (which studies and

With help from agencies in England, Canada, Australia, and New Zealand, the NSA runs a global spy system code-named ECHELON. Utilizing a series of satellites and earth stations, such as the one seen here outside of Munich, Germany, ECHELON monitors the world's telecommunication networks.

collects the messages sent within the signals), and the Office of Research and Engineering (which creates the equipment and methods used for intercepting transmissions, breaking codes, and securing U.S. codes).

Working for the NSA

Once NSA applicants complete the CAIP program, they are cryptanalysts. Cryptanalysts can branch out into related fields, such as intelligence analysis (actually

The cornerstone of Coca-Cola's success is its secret formula, which it has guarded from its competitors since 1886. Corporations keep their trade secrets nearly as aggressively as nations keep their military and intelligence secrets.

studying the information, rather than trying to make the information readable), computer science, and information security (protecting materials rather than encoding them or breaking codes). Most NSA employees start as cryptanalysts, and their careers can lead to high-level management and technical positions as well.

The NSA is still one of the best places for a cryptologist to work. It offers a strong community, with more cryptologists than any other U.S. company or agency. It also provides its employees with the latest in workstations, computers, and other cryptographic tools. NSA employees are even encouraged to develop their own software programs.

Corporate Encryption Security

What makes a company successful? Is it being more honest or friendlier than the competition? Not usually. Most successful companies offer products that people want at the right prices. To accomplish both, companies have trade secrets. Think of Kentucky Fried Chicken or Coca-Cola. Their trade secrets are the formulas that make their products taste the way they do, making people want to buy them. If a rival learns how to create the same product, it could beat the competition. Those trade secrets—the recipes, blueprints, and manufacturing tricks—are more valuable than gold or oil or diamonds.

That's where cryptologists come in. Corporations hire cryptologists for their in-house security. "It takes a thief to catch a thief" is the old saying. "It takes a crypto to stop a crypto" could be the new, high-tech saying. Afraid hackers are going to break into your

Bruce Schneier

Even though cryptologists work with secrets, their own identities might be public knowledge. Cryptologists like to meet one another and compare ideas, and they also share stories. Probably the most famous cryptologist today is Bruce Schneier. Born in Brooklyn, New York, Schneier received a degree in physics from the University of Rochester and a master's degree in computer science from American University in Washington, D.C. He worked for the Department of Defense for several years before leaving to form his own company, Counterpane Systems. Schneier is also the author of *Applied Cryptography* (published in 1993), one of the best basic texts about cryptology.

Schneier was a central figure during the Crypto Wars and actively campaigned to defend the right to use strong crypto. In 1999, immediately after the Crypto Wars ended, Schneier closed Counterpane Systems and created a new company, Counterpane Internet Security. The old company provided cryptology for its clients; the new company provides security against cryptanalysts. Counterpane focuses on protection through careful monitoring rather than through clever codes, and emphasizes the human element in its security systems.

mainframe and steal your secrets? They could intercept trade secrets in a message sent to your new manufacturing plant. To stop this threat, companies hire several hackers to build the defenses that protect important, secret information.

Encryption protection is particularly important in the modern world. Sixty years ago, even the largest companies had only one or two locations. That made it easy to keep the secrets safe. The formulas were locked in a large vault, and the company president personally mixed each batch of the formula or taught the chemists one at a time. Today, however, companies have locations all over the world, and most business is handled by fax, telephone, and e-mail. The trade secrets are sent more often, over greater distances, and to more people, than ever before. That makes them much more vulnerable, which increases the need for good protection.

The increase in remote and computerized systems also means more vulnerability. Sixty years ago, you took your paycheck to the bank and the teller deposited or cashed it for you. When you wanted more money, you went back to the bank and spoke to the teller again. Today your money is likely deposited automatically

With the increasing use of online transactions for business and personal finances, privacy has become more important than ever.

from your employer's bank account into your bank account. You go to an ATM machine, put in your card, type in your code, and take out your money. You buy things over the telephone or over the Internet, and read off or type in your credit card number. The information is being sent through systems rather than through people, and that makes it vulnerable.

Banks employ cryptologists for exactly this reason. They need to protect their money and to make certain the person spending it electronically is the person who owns that account. Hackers are always trying to break through banks' defenses, and cryptologists are there to prevent that. They build stronger systems—with stronger codes—to keep the unauthorized from gaining entry and stealing money or information.

Cable companies are also a major employer of cryptologists. Television signals are sent electronically to each home, either by cable or by satellite. The signals are encrypted so that only people who pay for the service can see the shows. But people are always finding ways to break the system and get cable for free. So, the cable companies hire cryptologists to build better encryptions and protect their assets.

Internet

Internet companies are another major employer of cryptologists. The Web is all about information. People across the world are constantly exchanging information. Sometimes they reveal more than they want. Internet purchases are a particularly vulnerable area. If you order a CD online, you need to type in your credit card information. What's to stop someone

In order to ensure that everyone is paying for what they watch, cable companies such as Adelphia Communications in Berlin, Vermont, encrypt their transmissions.

from intercepting that information and then using your credit card for purchases? If you look at the bottom of your browser, you'll usually see a small padlock icon. That indicates whether a site is secure. The locked padlock means the site is secure, because it encrypts all information. Your credit card information is sent in code so that a hacker cannot understand it.

Cryptologists build those systems and are constantly improving them to provide better security. They also build encoding systems like public-key encryption so that people can send messages privately and not worry about their messages being intercepted and read by someone else.

The Plaintext

Ultimately, cryptology is about patterns. Cryptographers build patterns to protect and conceal information. Cryptanalysts study patterns to break them apart and expose the information. It's a puzzle, and the key is figuring out how the pieces fit together. So, if you like

Before purchasing items online with a credit card, it is important to make sure that the site encrypts all the information submitted to it.

making puzzles or solving them, cryptology might be for you. Just remember that the content isn't important. You could be talking about homework, dinner, or a movie you just saw. Cryptologists care only about how the information is sent, how it's protected, and how it's revealed.

Glossary

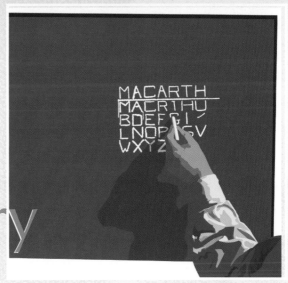

algorithm A mathematical procedure used to determine what replaces the letters in a cipher.

Alice, Bob, and Eve The three names traditionally used by cryptographers for their examples—Alice and Bob try to send secret messages to one another, and Eve tries to intercept the messages and crack the code.

cipher key A short piece of text (one to ten letters usually) used to encode and decode messages; also called a key.

cipher system An encryption system where one letter is replaced with another.

ciphertext Encoded text, which usually looks like gibberish.

code System that uses symbols or groups of letters to represent words or phrases.

codebook   A dictionary of code groups accompanied by their plaintext.

code group   Code words and their matching phrases or numbers.

code key   The system for translating plaintext into ciphertext, or vice versa.

cryptanalysis   The art of breaking secret codes.

crypto   Short for cryptography; usually refers to encryption systems.

cryptograms   Writings in cipher or code.

cryptographic systems   Devices for enciphering and deciphering.

cryptography   The art of making secret codes.

cryptology   The science of encoding and decoding information (includes both cryptanalysis and cryptography).

plaintext   Original, unencoded text, which is readable by humans; also called cleartext or plaincode.

polyalphabetic substitution   Any cipher system in which the characters are not always represented by the same cipher characters ("a" might become "f" one time but "g" another time and "h" a third time)

public-key encryption   An encryption method that uses openly available keys to encode but completely different keys to decode.

simple substitution   Any cipher system in which each character is always replaced by the same cipher character ("a" always becomes "f," "b" always becomes "g," etc.); also called monoalphabetic substitution

strong crypto   Cryptographic codes that are extremely hard to crack.

substitution cipher   A cipher where the letters of a word are exchanged for another set of letters.

transposition   A cipher where the letters of a word are shuffled around.

For More Information

Organizations

The American Cryptogram Association
Gary Rasmussen, ACA Treasurer
P.O. Box 1013
Londonderry, NH 03053-1013
Web site: http://www.cryptogram.org

Computer Security Institute (CSI)
600 Harrison Street
San Francisco, CA 94107
(415) 947-6320
Web site: http://www.gocsi.com

International Association for Cryptologic Research
IACR General Secretariat
Santa Rosa Administrative Center
University of California
Santa Barbara, CA 93106-6120
e-mail: iacrmem@iacr.org
Web site: http://www.iacr.org

National Security Agency (NSA)
NSA Public Affairs Office
(301) 688-6524
Web site: http://www.nsa.gov

Web Sites

Due to the changing nature of Internet links, the
Rosen Publishing Group, Inc., has developed an
online list of Web sites related to the subject of this
book. This site is updated regularly. Please use this
link to access the list:

http://www.rosenlinks.com/ec/cryp

For Further Reading

Durrett, Deanne. *Unsung Heroes of WWII: The Story of the Navajo Code Talkers.* New York: Facts on File, 1998.

Flannery, Sarah, and David Flannery. *In Code.* New York: Workman, 2001.

Fowler, Mark, and Radhi Parekh. *Codes & Ciphers* (Usborne Superpuzzles: Advanced Level). Chicago: EDC, 1995.

Gardner, Martin. *Codes, Ciphers and Secret Writing.* London: Dover, 1984.

James, Elizabeth. *How to Keep a Secret: Writing and Talking in Code.* Chicago: Morrow, 1998.

Miller, Marvin, and Jim Frazier. *How to Write and Decode Secret Messages.* New York: Scholastic, 1998.

Reynard, Robert. *Secret Code Breaker: A Cryptanalyst's Handbook*. Chicago: Smith & Daniel, 1996.

Singh, Simon. *The Code Book: How to Make It, Break It, Hack It, Crack It*. New York: Delacorte Press, 2002.

Singh, Simon. *Code Book: The Science of Secrecy from Ancient Egypt to Quantum Cryptography*. New York: Random House, 2000.

Wrixon, Fred B. *Codes and Ciphers*. New York: Wiley, 1992.

Bibliography

Bury, Jan. "Crypto Machines." Retrieved August 25, 2002 (http://webhome.idirect.com/~jproc/crypto/menu.html).

Bury, Jan. "The Greatest Secret of World War II—The Enigma Code Breach." Retrieved August 25, 2002 (http://webhome.idirect.com/~jproc/crypto/enigma.html).

"Codes, Ciphers, & Codebreaking." Retrieved August 24, 2002 (http://www.vectorsite.net/ttcode1.html#m1).

Dasgupta, Partha. "Making and Breaking Codes." Retrieved August 22, 2002 (http://cactus.eas.asu.edu/partha/Columns/03-19-encryption.htm).

DODD 5010.10 Intelligence Career Development Program. Retrieved August 21, 2002 (http://www.fas.org/irp/doddir/dod/dodcar.htm).

International Association for Cryptologic Research. Retrieved August 19, 2002 (http://www.iacr.org).

Kallis, Stephen A., Jr. "Codes and Ciphers." Retrieved August 30, 2002 (http://www.otr.com/ciphers.html).

Mann, Charles C. "Homeland Insecurity." *Atlantic Monthly*, Vol. 290, No. 2, September 2002, pp. 81–102.

Menzin, Margaret, and Robert Goldman. "Careers in Mathematics." Association for Women in Mathematics. Retrieved August 24, 2002 (http://math.usask.ca/document/netinfo/careers.html).

meta4. "The National Security Agency: The Secret Unveiled . . . 05.15.00." cipherwar.com. Retrieved August 21, 2002 (http://www.cipherwar.com/news/00/meta4_nsa.htm).

National Cryptologic Museum. Retrieved August 20, 2002 (http://www.nsa.gov/museum/index.html).

National Security Agency "Cryptanalysis: Mastering the Mysteries and the Mental Challenges." Retrieved August 24, 2002 (http://www.nsa.gov/programs/employ/index.html).

Navy and Marine Corps WWII Commemorative Committee. "Navajo Code Talkers of World War II." Retrieved August 21, 2002 (http://webhome. idirect.com/~jproc/crypto/codetalk.html).

Professional Development—Cryptology (Naval). Retrieved August 24, 2002 (http://www.fas.org/irp/agency/navy/bupers/ pers-4/pers-44/pers4410/prfsnl.htm).

Sharpe, Andrew R. W. "How Mathematics Saved the World: The Allies' Decryption Efforts During World War II." Retrieved August 21, 2002 (http://personal. nbnet.nb.ca/michaels/hist3300.htm).

TotalJobs.com. "So You Want to be a Cryptologist?" Retrieved August 26, 2002 (http://www.totaljobs. com/editorial/getadvice_wannabe/cryptologist.shtm).

Weadon, Patrick D. "Cryptologic History and NSA: 'Follow the Drinking Gourd.'" National Security Agency. Retrieved August 22, 2002. (http://www.nsa.gov/docs/history/index.html).

"The World's First Cryptomachine." Retrieved August 26, 2002 (http://hem.passagen.se/tan01/grip.html).

Index

About the Author

Aaron Rosenberg was born in New Jersey, grew up in New Orleans, and now lives in New York. He has taught college-level English and worked in corporate graphics, and now runs his own role-playing game publishing company (www.clockworksgames.com). He has written short stories, essays, poems, articles, novels, and role-playing games.

Photo Credits

Cover © Bob Rowan/Prgressive Image/Corbis; pp. 5, 24, 28, 39, 42, 46, 48 © AP/Wide World Photos; p. 7 © AKG London; pp. 8, 12 © Corbis; pp. 9, 11 © Hulton/Archive/Getty Images, Inc.; p. 19 © Bettmann/Corbis; p. 22 © Tria Giovan/Corbis; p.31 © Philip Gould/Corbis; p. 32 © Palmer/Kane, Inc./Corbis; p. 34 © Thom Lang/Corbis; p. 37 © Richard Moore/U.S. Navy/Getty Images, Inc.; p. 41 © Michael Dalder/Reuters/Timepix; p. 50 © Dex Images/Corbis.

Designer: Les Kanturek; Editor: Mark Beyer